SUPERSTARS
of
PRO
FOOTBALL

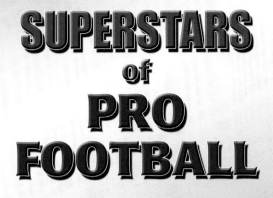

H. H. Lourdes-Pitt

Mason Crest Publishers
Philadelphia

MASON CREST PUBLISHERS, INC.
370 Reed Road
Broomall PA 19008
(866) MCP-BOOK (toll free)
www.masoncrest.com

Printed in the United States of America.

CPISA compliance information: Batch#060110-FB2. For further information, contact Mason Crest Publishers at 610-543-6200.

First printing

9 8 7 6 5 4 3 2 1

Library of Congress Cataloging-in-Publication Data

Lourdes-Pitt, H. H.
  Brett Favre / H. H. Lourdes-Pitt.
      p. cm. — (Superstars of pro football)
  Includes bibliographical references and index.
ISBN 978-1-4222-1662-0 (hc)
ISBN 978-1-4222-1982-9 (pb)
 1. Favre, Brett-   Juvenile literature. 2. Football players—United States—Biography—Juvenile literature. 3. Quarterbacks (Football)—United States—Biography—Juvenile literature. I. Title.
GV939.F29L68 2010
796.332092—dc22
[B]   2010015964

‹‹ C R O S S - C U R R E N T S ››

In the ebb and flow of the currents of life we are each influenced by many people, places, and events that we directly experience or have learned about. Throughout the chapters of this book you will come across CROSS-CURRENTS reference bubbles. These bubbles direct you to a CROSS-CURRENTS section in the back of the book that contains fascinating and informative articles and related pictures. Go on. ››

◀◀ CONTENTS ▶▶

THE 40-YEAR-OLD KID

Kids across the United States love to play football, whether this means tossing the **pigskin** around with friends in backyards or neighborhood streets, participating in Pop Warner youth leagues, or suiting up with a high school team. Football is a fun, action-packed game. It is also America's most popular spectator sport.

But there is no denying that the National Football League (NFL) is also a big business. NFL **franchises** are worth hundreds of millions of dollars. TV networks pay *billions* of dollars to obtain the rights to broadcast the NFL's games.

All NFL players receive excellent salaries. In 2009, the lowest-paid **rookies** in the league earned seven times more than the average American worker. **Veterans** earn more still, and stars take home millions of dollars each year.

But one thing must be emphasized about salaries in the NFL. Because football is such a rough sport, an injury can end a player's career—and his paychecks—at any time. In fact, the average NFL career lasts only about three years. It is no wonder, then, that many players approach football more as a job than as a game.

For Love of the Game

Brett Favre is not like other NFL players. For one thing, his durability has defied the odds. From early in the 1992 season—when he first became a starting quarterback—through 2009, Brett never missed a single start. That's nearly 18 full seasons, including playoffs, without being sidelined by an injury. The amazing streak is a testament to Brett's incredible toughness.

Equally remarkable, Brett has never lost his enthusiasm for the game. It always looks like he's having fun on the field, because he is.

In a 2007 interview, Brett was asked whether he would play in the NFL if he didn't get paid. "Yes," he replied. "I love to play football."

The answer may have sounded unbelievable. But few fans who had followed Brett's professional career closely could doubt his sincerity. Skeptics who watched him in action on January 17, 2010, had good reason to become believers as well. That day, Brett's Minnesota Vikings went up against the Dallas Cowboys in the divisional playoffs of the National Football Conference (NFC). The winner would earn a trip to the NFC championship game.

A sellout crowd of 63,000 was rocking the Metrodome in Minneapolis when the teams took the field for the 1:00 P.M. opening kickoff. Nearly 11 minutes had elapsed on the game clock before the Vikings' fans got a

CROSS-CURRENTS
To learn more about the way in which the National Football League is organized, read "Conferences and Divisions." See page 46.

Brett Favre of the Minnesota Vikings launches a touchdown pass during Minnesota's January 2010 playoff game against the Dallas Cowboys. Over the course of his long career, Brett has established himself as one of the greatest passers in NFL history. He holds many league records for quarterbacks.

taste of what they'd come for, as Minnesota wide receiver Sidney Rice hauled in a perfectly thrown Brett Favre **bomb** and scooted into the end zone for a 47-yard touchdown. At age 40, Brett was almost old enough to be the 23-year-old Rice's father. But the wide receiver couldn't match his quarterback's enthusiasm in celebrating the TD. Brett, knocked down by Cowboys linebacker Anthony Spencer right after he released the ball, bounced to his feet, jumped into the air for a chest bump with running back Naufahu Tahi, then fist-pumped his way to the sideline. After high-fiving a teammate there, he jabbed his right arm toward one end of the Metrodome, then wheeled and jabbed toward the other end. The hometown crowd went wild.

The Metrodome had more to celebrate in the second quarter, when Brett connected with Rice for another touchdown. This one, from 16 yards out, gave Minnesota a 17–3 lead at halftime.

Midway through the fourth quarter, now up by a score of 20–3, the Vikings had the ball at the Cowboys' 45-yard line. Facing third-and-4, Brett threw deep. Again his target was Rice, who beat his man and waltzed across the goal line for his third touchdown of the game. Arms raised, Brett made a beeline for the end zone. Along the way, he jumped on the back of teammate Anthony Herrera, riding the 315-pound offensive guard like a jockey. After dismounting, Brett found Rice, still in the end zone, and hugged the young receiver. In his exuberance, the quarterback didn't look much like a 19-year veteran who had thrown close to 500 TD passes in his professional career. He looked more like a nine-year-old kid celebrating his first Pop Warner touchdown.

Brett performed another round of fist pumps, chest bumps, and high fives after his fourth touchdown pass of the game. The 11-yarder, to tight end Visanthe Shiancoe, came with just 1:55 left on the game clock. It wrapped up the Vikings' 34–3 dismantling of Dallas. Asked about his high-spirited celebrations throughout the contest, Brett said:

Brett congratulates Sidney Rice after the wide receiver caught a 45-yard touchdown during the 2010 playoff game against Dallas. It was Rice's third touchdown reception of the game.

Brett salutes fans at the Metrodome after the Vikings' 34–3 divisional playoff beat-down of the Cowboys, January 17, 2010. The victory made Brett the first quarterback in NFL history to win a postseason game after turning 40.

"As long as I'm out there, the enthusiasm and the passion that you see is real. And I know the guys feed off of that. Fans enjoy that, because it is real and genuine."

Minnesota's victory over Dallas had made Brett the first quarterback age 40 or older ever to win an NFL playoff game. That milestone didn't seem too significant, though—considering that he played the game with the enthusiasm of a kid.

MISSISSIPPI ROOTS

Brett Lorenzo Favre was born on October 10, 1969, at Memorial Hospital in Gulfport, Mississippi. He was the second child of Irvin and Bonita Favre, joining older brother Scott. The boys' father, Irvin "Big Irv" Favre, was a high school teacher and football coach. Their mother, Bonita, was a special-education teacher. Eventually the Favre family would come to include another boy, Jeff, and a girl, Brandi.

Born on the Bayou

The Favres lived in Kiln, a community of fewer than 2,000 people located in southern Mississippi's Hancock County. An hour's drive from New Orleans, Kiln (pronounced "Kill" by

When Brett was growing up, he hunted, fished, and played with his brothers and friends in the bayou near his Mississippi home.

residents) was in a very rural area. The town didn't have a single traffic light, and its "downtown" consisted of a pair of gas stations and a bar.

Kiln is in the Gulf Coast's **bayou** country, where the low-lying land is laced with marshes, lakes, and very slow moving creeks and rivers. The Favres' modest ranch house sat on a secluded 52-acre tract of woodlands and meadows between Mill Creek and Rotten Bayou. With no neighbors close by, the three Favre brothers and a cousin, David Peterson, were one another's constant companions as children. They hunted in the woods, swam and fished in the bayou, and pelted each other with rocks inside an old barn on the Favres' property. Their roughhousing often left the boys bruised and bleeding, but they loved it.

"We was wild," Peterson recalled.

"It's probably a good thing we didn't live in the city because we would have tore things up."

A Natural

Big Irv Favre, who coached American Legion baseball as well as football, loved sports. And from an early age so did his son Brett. Brett's legendary toughness was apparent from an early age as well. When he was four years old and playing baseball, Brett got hit in the head with a bat. The blow raised a big welt, and Brett had to be taken to the hospital. "He didn't even cry," Irv Favre recalled.

"The doctor said it hurt the woman who took him to the hospital more than it hurt Brett."

Throughout his grade school years, Brett played football. But it wasn't until he reached fifth grade that he got his first chance to play quarterback. He had an incredibly strong arm. One of his teachers, Billy Ray Dedeaux, would recall that Brett was throwing 50-yard passes as a fifth-grader. Still, he wasn't very accurate, and his coach, Rocky Gaudin, insists that he coached kids who were better quarterbacks than Brett as youngsters.

Brett was thought to have more potential as a baseball player. In 1982, while still in eighth grade, he started at third base for the varsity team at Hancock North Central High School. Not only that, but he led the team in batting average.

High School Years

When Brett entered Hancock North Central as a student in 1983, his brother Scott, a senior, was quarterback of the football team. So Brett bided his time as an offensive lineman and, on defense, a safety. He was also the punter and placekicker.

Irvin Favre was Hancock North Central's head football coach. Big Irv was a strict disciplinarian. He made his players work extremely hard, and he didn't want to hear any grumbling. The strong work ethic and no-excuses approach that Brett has displayed

Brett poses with his father, Irvin Favre, in Green Bay's famous Lambeau Field. Big Irv was Brett's high school football coach.

throughout his pro career were formed under the watchful eye of his father.

In the spring of his freshman year, Brett again starred on the baseball diamond. Once more he led the team in hitting, as he would in each of his high school years.

Brett's sophomore year brought a major disappointment. A case of **mononucleosis** forced him to sit out the football season. Off the **gridiron**, however, good things were happening in Brett's social life. Brett was by nature a shy person, but for a year he'd been dating Deanna Tynes, who was also born and raised in Kiln. The two had first met in 1976, in a Catholic catechism class. Brett had been seven and Deanna eight. Now they were nearly inseparable—though they weren't typical high school sweethearts. For her birthday one year Brett bought her a catcher's mitt and mask. Deanna recalled:

> **"The thing we had in common was sports. Our 'dates' were not what you'd call exciting—we played catch a lot."**

Brett finally got his chance to play quarterback during his junior year of high school. Outside of Hancock North Central, no one really took notice. That's because the coach rarely let him throw. Big Irv had once attended a coaching clinic held by Paul "Bear" Bryant, the University of Alabama's legendary head coach. Bryant championed the "wishbone," an offensive scheme in which three running backs lined up in the backfield and the vast majority of plays were rushes. Big Irv came away from the clinic a big believer in the wishbone. His teams would rush the ball on almost every play—and he wasn't about to change his offensive philosophy just because his son was the quarterback. Brett seldom threw more than five passes in a game.

CROSS-CURRENTS

In his 38 years as a college head football coach, Paul "Bear" Bryant had 37 winning seasons. For more information about Bryant's life and career, see page 47.

Brett completed his junior season without attracting any attention from college football recruiters. He was in the middle of his senior

This November 1986 photo shows Brett getting a rare chance to throw the ball during a high school game. At Hancock North Central High, Irvin Favre only allowed his son to pass a few times each game.

season, still without a single scholarship offer, when his dad decided to take matters into his own hands. Big Irv had attended the University of Southern Mississippi, where he'd been a baseball star, and he used some connections to have Brett scouted. Mark McHale, the offensive line coach at Southern Miss, went to see a Hancock North Central game. But Big Irv stuck to his usual game plan, and Brett only threw the ball a few times.

McHale hadn't seen enough to convince him that the young man from Kiln deserved a football scholarship. He did, however, agree to check out another game. Again Brett threw just a handful of passes, but McHale thought he played pretty well on defense at the safety position. Southern Miss offered its last available football scholarship to Brett, making clear that he would be groomed as a defensive back. With no offers from other colleges, Brett accepted. He planned to major in special education at Southern Miss.

Hero of Hattiesburg

In the summer of 1987, Brett traveled to Hattiesburg, about 50 miles north of Kiln, to attend Southern Mississippi's football camp. He begged to be given a shot at the quarterback position, and the Golden Eagles' coaching staff agreed, penciling him in as the seventh QB on their depth chart. It would take exactly one practice for Brett to begin moving up on the list. "The first morning, I was standing with my back to his group," Southern Miss head coach Jim Carmody recalled.

"I heard this noise, a whooshing sound. I turned around and said, 'What in the world is that?'"

It was the sound of a Brett Favre pass, flying through the air like a bullet. Carmody couldn't believe how powerful Brett's arm was. By the beginning of the season, the 17-year-old kid from Kiln was the Golden Eagles' third-string quarterback.

In the season's second week, with his offense struggling and his team trailing Tulane in the second half, Carmody decided it was time to see what Brett could do in a game situation. The

Brett looks for an open receiver during the first game of his junior season at the University of Southern Mississippi. The September 1989 game marked one of the highlights of Brett's college career, as he led the Golden Eagles to a 30–26 upset victory over the nationally ranked Florida Seminoles.

freshman responded by throwing two touchdown passes and engineering a come-from-behind victory. From that point on, Brett was the Golden Eagles' starting quarterback for the next four years.

Southern Miss was no football powerhouse, but Brett would lead the team to a 29–17 record, including two bowl victories, in his four years at Hattiesburg. Several of his performances have become the stuff of legend at Southern Miss. One came in the season opener of 1989, Brett's junior year. The Golden Eagles traveled to Gainesville, Florida, to face Florida State University. The Seminoles were ranked sixth in the nation. Late in the game, with his team trailing by a score of 26–24, Brett drove Southern Miss the length of the field. He threw the game-winning touchdown pass with just 23 seconds left on the clock.

Topsy-Turvy

By the time his late-game heroics stunned the mighty Seminoles, Brett's personal life had been turned upside down. In February 1989, Deanna Tynes had given birth to a daughter, Brittany. Deanna was only 20 years old, and Brett just 19. "We had no idea where our lives were going," Deanna said. Neither felt ready to marry. Deanna dropped out of college, found work waiting tables and cleaning bathrooms, and raised Brittany as a single mom. Brett, meanwhile, stayed at Southern Miss. Whenever he could, he traveled to Kiln to see Deanna and Brittany.

Brett's life took another unexpected—and nearly tragic—turn on the evening of July 14, 1960. Brett, his brother Scott, and a friend had spent the day fishing. On the way back to Kiln, Brett lost control of his car on a winding gravel road. The car ran into a ditch and flipped over. Had Scott not been following his brother in his pickup truck, Brett would probably have died. Scott used a golf club to break a window and drag Brett out of the car. He then called an ambulance. Brett, who had suffered a concussion, cracked vertebrae, and internal injuries, was put in the intensive care unit at the hospital.

Three weeks later, doctors had to surgically remove more than 30 inches of Brett's small intestine. It seemed he would miss his senior season. He missed one game.

To the astonishment of everyone, including his Southern Miss teammates, Brett led the Golden Eagles onto the field at Alabama's Bryant-Denny Stadium on September 8. Then he led the team to a 27–24, come-from-behind upset victory. Of that game, Alabama head coach Gene Stallings would say later:

"You can call it a miracle or a legend or whatever you want to. I just know that on that day, Brett Favre was larger than life."

Despite his amazing toughness and determination, the effects of the car accident hampered Brett's play during his senior season. Still, he led the Golden Eagles to an 8–4 record and a berth in the All-American Bowl. Southern Miss lost that game to North Carolina State, 31–24, but Brett came up big in his final collegiate outing. He threw for 341 yards, including three touchdowns, and was named Most Valuable Player (MVP) of the game.

When he left Southern Miss in 1991, Brett had established numerous school records. They included most career pass attempts, completions, passing yards, passing percentage, and touchdowns. The NFL beckoned.

MVP
TIMES THREE

O n April 21, 1991, the NFL's annual draft got under way in New York City with the Dallas Cowboys taking linebacker Russell Maryland with the first overall pick. Two quarterbacks were drafted in the first round, but Brett Favre wasn't one of them. The Atlanta Falcons made Brett the sixth player chosen in the second round—the 33rd overall pick.

Even that low in the draft, Atlanta head coach Jerry Glanville had been against the decision to take Brett. But the team's general manager, Ken Herock, had prevailed.

Glanville and Brett never got along. During one preseason game, the coach famously said that it would take a plane crash for him to put Brett in the game. Brett didn't help his cause by showing up late to practices and falling asleep at team meetings. He also began drinking a lot.

The 1991 season turned out to be a complete washout for Brett. He saw brief action in just two games, failing to complete a pass.

Two of his four pass attempts were intercepted, and one of those picks was run back for a touchdown.

CROSS-CURRENTS

For general information about how the NFL draft works, along with some interesting details about the 1991 draft, turn to page 48.

By season's end, the relationship between Brett and Glanville seemed beyond repair. Plus, Brett had behaved irresponsibly and unprofessionally. Ken Herock decided he had to unload the young quarterback. In February 1992, Atlanta traded Brett to the Green Bay Packers for a first-round draft pick.

The Lambeau Legend Begins

Green Bay was a proud franchise that had fallen on hard times. The team had suffered through a miserable 1991 season, finishing with a record of 4–12. In four of the five seasons before that, the Packers had also posted losing records. First-year head coach Mike Holmgren hoped to turned things around in 1992.

Green Bay entered the 1992 season with Don "Majik Man" Majkowski as its starting quarterback. Brett Favre was Majkowski's backup.

In week 3, a home game against the Cincinnati Bengals, the Majik Man went down early with an ankle injury. Holmgren sent Brett in to replace him.

The second-year pro got off to a rocky start. He fumbled four times, and as the fourth quarter began, the Packers were looking at the short end of a 17–3 score. Fans at Green Bay's Lambeau Field started calling for Ty Detmer, the Packers' third-string quarterback. Brett quieted them down a bit by putting together a scoring drive that he capped off with a five-yard touchdown pass to wide receiver Sterling Sharpe.

Then, with 1:07 left in the game, the real excitement began. Green Bay trailed, 23–17, and was pinned deep in its own territory. The Packers got a big play when Brett connected with Sharpe for 42 yards. With 13 seconds left in the game, Brett threw a 35-yard touchdown pass to wide receiver Kitrick Taylor, giving Green Bay a 24–23 victory.

With that thrilling performance, Brett won over the Cheeseheads, Green Bay's famously dedicated football fans. He also won the job as the Packers' starting quarterback. He would remain number one—on Green Bay's QB depth chart and in the hearts of Cheeseheads—for more than 15 years.

The Price of Fame

By the end of the 1992 football season, Brett Favre was the toast of Green Bay. At just 23 years old and in his first season as an NFL starter, Brett

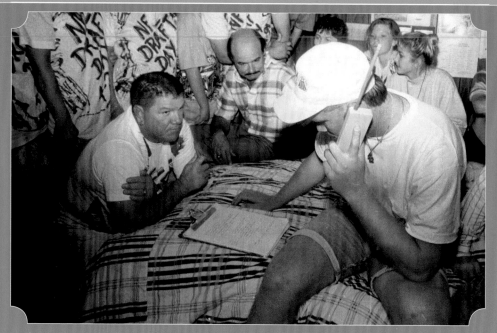

Irvin Favre watches his son answer a call from the Atlanta Falcons on NFL draft day, April 1991. Brett was chosen in the second round of that year's draft.

had been voted to the **Pro Bowl**. More important, his strong right arm and gambling, seat-of-the-pants style of play had rejuvenated the Packers' offense. After dropping its first two games, the team had finished with a 9–7 record. Cheeseheads were eagerly anticipating the 1993 campaign.

Brett returned home to Mississippi during the off-season. There, he and Deanna Tynes tried to sort out their relationship. Eventually they decided that Deanna and three-year-old Brittany should join Brett in Green Bay for the 1993 season.

When she went to Green Bay, Deanna was surprised at how much Brett had changed. He'd always been easygoing, reserved around people he didn't know well, and a bit of a homebody. Now he frequently stayed out all night, and when he was home, he often brooded or lashed out at Deanna. Gradually she recognized the cause of Brett's behavior—he'd become addicted to Vicodin, a powerful painkiller. Deanna explained:

CROSS-CURRENTS

The Green Bay Packers are unique among pro sports franchises in the United States. To find out why, turn to page 50.

Brett throws a 35-yard touchdown pass during the fourth quarter of his second NFL appearance with the Packers, September 20, 1992. Although Brett started slowly, he finished the day with 289 passing yards and two touchdowns, leading Green Bay to a come-from-behind victory over the Cincinnati Bengals.

"All of a sudden, he was thrust into the spotlight. He was shy. Whether it was Vicodin or alcohol, that was his way of coping."

Despite his struggles with substance abuse, Brett managed to perform well on the gridiron. Although he threw 24 interceptions in 1993, he also made a lot of big plays, leading the Packers to another 9–7 record and their first postseason appearance in more than a decade. The Packers knocked off the Detroit Lions in the **wild card** game, then fell to the Dallas Cowboys in the divisional playoff round.

Brett turned in a great 1994 season, throwing 33 touchdown passes against only 14 interceptions. For the Packers, 1994 played out like a rerun of 1993: a 9–7 regular-season record, a wild card win over the Lions, a loss to the Cowboys in the divisional playoffs.

CROSS-CURRENTS

The Pro Bowl matches a team f NFC all-stars against a team of AFC all-stars. For more information, turn to page 51.

The Packers compiled an 11–5 regular-season record and got one step closer to the Super Bowl in 1995, reaching the NFC championship game. For the third straight year, however, the Dallas Cowboys ended Green Bay's season.

What a season it had been for Brett Favre. Brett staked his claim to the title of best quarterback in the NFL. He threw a league-leading 38 touchdown passes—including a record-tying 99-yarder to wide receiver Robert Brooks—while getting intercepted just 13 times. He also led the league in passing yardage (4,413). His breakout season earned Brett a spot on the NFL's **All-Pro** team as well as league MVP honors.

To legions of Cheeseheads, along with football fans around the country, Brett seemed to have everything going for him. But on May 14, 1996, at a press conference at Lambeau Field, he announced that he was dependent on painkillers and would be checking himself into a **rehab** facility.

Brett spent six weeks at the Menninger Clinic in Topeka, Kansas. After he completed his treatment, he went back to Mississippi. There, on July 14, he and Deanna were married.

Super Bowl Season

Led by their newlywed quarterback, the Packers got off to a blazing start during the 1996 season. They won eight of their first nine games before suffering consecutive losses to the Kansas City Chiefs and Dallas Cowboys in weeks 11 and 12.

But then Brett and his teammates went on a tear, winning five straight games to finish the regular season at 13–3, tied with the Denver Broncos for best record in the NFL. Brett again led the league in touchdown passes, with 39. For the second consecutive year he was voted an All-Pro. He also won league MVP honors for the second straight time, joining San Francisco 49ers legend Joe Montana as the only player ever to accomplish that feat.

Those individual honors couldn't replace the ultimate football experience, however. Brett—along with his Packers teammates and the entire city of Green Bay—thirsted for a Super Bowl championship.

The Packers, who had earned a first-round bye, hosted the 49ers in the divisional playoffs. To the delight of the sellout crowd at Lambeau Field, Green Bay scored the first three touchdowns of the game and coasted to a 35–14 victory.

In the NFC championship game, against the Carolina Panthers, Brett was shaky in the early going. He turned the ball over twice, on a fumble and an interception. Carolina held a 10–7 lead in the second quarter, but then Brett got Green Bay's offense untracked. His 292 passing yards and two touchdown throws paced the Packers to a 30–13 victory—and earned them a trip to New Orleans for Super Bowl XXXI.

More than 72,000 fans packed the Louisiana Superdome on January 26, 1997, for the matchup between the NFC-champion Packers and the New England Patriots, champions of the American Football Conference (AFC). Brett wasted little time in getting his team on the board. On Green Bay's second play from scrimmage, he went deep to wide receiver Andre Rison. The 54-yard touchdown pass gave the Packers a 7–0 lead. A couple minutes later, Green Bay added a field goal to go up by 10 points.

But New England fought back. By the end of the first quarter, the Patriots held a 14–10 edge on the strength of two touchdown passes by QB Drew Bledsoe.

Less than a minute had elapsed in the second quarter when Brett dropped back to pass from the Green Bay 19-yard line. He launched a bomb to wide receiver Antonio Freeman. Freeman hauled in the perfectly thrown pass and scampered into the end zone. The 81-

Deanna and Brett Favre on their wedding day, July 14, 1996. Also pictured are Deanna's mother, Ann Tynes (left), and Brett's mother, Bonita Favre (right).

Brett dives toward the end zone for a two-yard touchdown during Super Bowl XXXI, January 26, 1997. Brett also threw for 246 yards and two touchdowns, leading Green Bay to victory over the New England Patriots, 35–21.

yard hookup set a record for the longest touchdown pass in Super Bowl history.

Green Bay got a field goal and another touchdown, on a two-yard Brett Favre run, to take a 27–14 halftime lead. The Packers went on to win, 35–21.

After the presentation of the Vince Lombardi Trophy, in the midst of the Packers' celebration, Brett said:

"We're champions today because we overcame a lot of adversity."

Brett was talking about the team, but he could just as easily have been referring to himself.

Another Outstanding Year

If anyone predicted that the Super Bowl champion Green Bay Packers or their two-time MVP quarterback would suffer a letdown in 1997, they were wrong. Green Bay

CROSS-CURRENTS

The Super Bowl is pro football's biggest stage. For an overview of the game's origins, turn to page 52.

again compiled a regular-season mark of 13–3. That was tied with the San Francisco 49ers and Kansas City Chiefs for best record in the league. Brett threw a league-high 35 touchdown passes. He was the co-winner—along with Detroit Lions running back Barry Sanders—of the NFL's MVP award, becoming the first player to earn that honor three consecutive years.

The Packers entered the 1997 postseason with a lot of momentum, having rattled off five straight victories to finish the regular season. After a first-round bye, Green Bay played host to the Tampa Bay Buccaneers in the divisional playoffs. The warm-weather Bucs didn't have much fun on the frozen tundra of Lambeau Field, falling by a score of 21–7.

The following week, Brett and his teammates went on the road to face the San Francisco 49ers in the NFC championship game. They emerged with a 23–10 victory.

Super Bowl XXXII, held in San Diego on January 25, 1998, pitted the Packers against the Denver Broncos. Brett played well, completing 25 of 42 passes for 256 yards, with three touchdowns and one interception. But Broncos running back Terrell Davis stole the show, rushing for 157 yards and three TDs. Davis's third score came with just 1:45 left in the fourth quarter. On the Packers' last possession, Brett drove his team to Denver's 31-yard line with four straight completions. But Denver's defense held, and the Broncos secured a 31–24 victory.

After the game, Brett, Deanna, and Brittany went to dinner with Deanna's sister and her husband. During the quiet meal, Deanna would later relate, Brett turned to her and said, "Thank God. Thank God I have you and Brittany." He had finally begun to understand, Deanna believed, that football wasn't the most important thing in the world. Family was more important.

Over the next several years, that lesson would be driven home again and again.

LOVE AND LOSS

In the spring of 1999, Deanna was pregnant with the Favres' second child. This should have been a time of anticipation and joy. Instead, conflict was roiling the Favres' marriage. Although Brett had overcome his addiction to painkillers three years earlier, he had not given up alcohol. And lately his drinking had gotten out of hand.

Matters came to a head when Brett's younger brother, Jeff, got married in Mississippi. After the wedding reception, Brett went on a two-day drinking binge with some of his old friends. When he finally showed up at his and Deanna's home in Hattiesburg, Brett found all his clothes packed in suitcases that were piled outside the house. Deanna had also contacted a divorce lawyer.

Brett and Deanna Favre in a happy moment. The high school sweethearts have remained together through many challenges, including Brett's struggles with addiction to painkilling drugs and alcohol and Deanna's battle against breast cancer.

Brett begged her to give him another chance, but she insisted that he leave and called his agent to pick him up. When the agent arrived, Brett told him to drive to the airport, because Brett was checking himself into rehab again. In her 2007 memoir, *Don't Bet Against Me!*, Deanna recalled:

> **Brett realized that if he wanted a life with me and the children, he couldn't drink again. He gave it up completely, and it's been eight years since he's had a drink.**

In July 1999, Deanna gave birth to another daughter. The Favres named her Breleigh.

Lean Times at Lambeau

The 1999 season started off well enough for Brett Favre and the Green Bay Packers. Despite an injured thumb on his throwing hand, Brett connected for four touchdown passes in the season opener, against the Oakland Raiders. The fourth TD came with just 11 seconds left on the game clock, giving the Packers a come-from-behind, 28–24 victory.

On November 7, 1999, Brett reached a milestone. He started his 117th straight game. This broke the NFL mark for consecutive starts by a quarterback, which was previously held by Ron Jaworski of the Philadelphia Eagles.

Overall, however, the 1999 season was a disappointment for Brett. He threw 22 touchdowns and 23 interceptions. Green Bay struggled to an 8–8 record and missed the playoffs.

The 2000 season wasn't much better. Brett recorded 20 touchdowns and was picked 16 times. To the disappointment of the Cheeseheads, the Packers again missed the playoffs, mustering a record of just 9–7.

Comeback

Some football observers began to wonder whether, at age 31, Brett Favre was over the hill. The Green Bay Packers didn't think so.

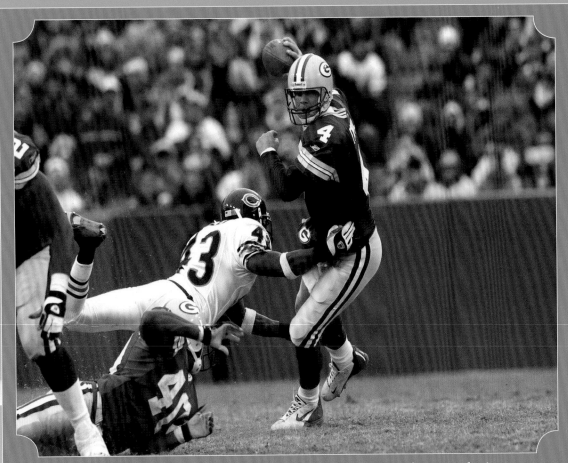

Blitzing Chicago Bears safety Mike Green can't quite catch Brett during a 2002 game in Green Bay. That season Brett completed nearly 62 percent of his passes for 3,658 yards and 27 touchdowns. He led the Packers to a 12–4 record and the NFC North title.

CROSS-CURRENTS

The NFL's salary cap was instituted in 1994 to help team owners contain payroll costs. For details on the cap and other information about player salaries, see page 53.

In February 2001, the team signed Brett to a long-term contract. On paper, the deal was for 10 years and would pay Brett $100 million. However, the contract was spread out to keep the Packers under the **salary cap**. Realistically it meant that Brett would be in Green Bay for six more years. But that was as long as he envisioned playing.

In announcing Brett's new contract, Packers general manager and head coach Mike Sherman said:

"No player in the NFL identifies or is more closely linked to a specific team like Brett Favre is to the Green Bay Packers. He embodies the spirit and character of Packers fans everywhere. I do not think there is a player in the NFL that experiences a relationship with the fans like Brett Favre does. That is very, very special."

Brett rewarded the team's confidence—and got Cheeseheads excited again—by turning in a marvelous 2001 season. He recorded 32 touchdown passes while limiting his interceptions to 15. Behind Brett's leadership, the Packers posted a regular-season record of 12–4 and beat the San Francisco 49ers in the wild card round of the playoffs. But the St. Louis Rams brought Green Bay's season to a screeching halt on January 20, 2002, beating the Packers by a score of 45–17 in the divisional playoffs. Rams defenders victimized Brett for six interceptions, returning three for touchdowns. It was arguably the worst performance of his pro career. But after the game, perhaps reflecting his changed perspective on football and on life, Brett was philosophical. He said:

"It's not the end of the world. We'll be back. I'll be back."

Brett did, in fact, come back with a fine 2002 season. He threw for 27 touchdowns against only 16 interceptions. Green Bay again finished the regular season with a 12–4 record, good enough for first place in the NFC North Division. Unfortunately, the Packers got bounced from the postseason in the wild card game, suffering a 27–7 defeat at the hands of the Atlanta Falcons.

Inspired by Irv

In 2003, Brett Favre threw 32 touchdown passes, leading the NFL in that category for the first time in a half-dozen years. But one remarkable performance would embody Brett's spirit and courage.

Packers head coach Mike Sherman congratulates Brett after the quarterback's fourth touchdown pass in a *Monday Night Football* game against the Oakland Raiders, December 22, 2003. Brett and his receivers dedicated their performance that night to the memory of Irvin Favre, who had died the day before.

After week 15, Green Bay's record stood at 8–6. With two games left in the regular season, the team was fighting for a spot in the playoffs. The schedule had the Packers traveling to Oakland for a week 16 showdown with the Raiders. That game would be telecast nationally on the popular *Monday Night Football* series.

On the evening of December 21, one day before Green Bay's game with Oakland, Irvin Favre suffered a heart attack and died. Big Irv was 58 years old.

Brett was in Oakland when he received the news. At an emotional team meeting, he announced that he would play in the Monday night game before heading to Mississippi for the funeral. His receiving corps promised they would catch any pass that was even in the general vicinity. That's pretty much what happened. Both the quarterback and his receivers played an inspired game. Brett completed 22 of 30 passes for 399 yards and four touchdowns, and Green Bay cruised to a 41–7 victory.

After the first TD, a 22-yard pass to tight end Wesley Walls, the quarterback and pass catcher embraced in the end zone. "I just said, 'I love you,' " Walls recounted after the game.

"He played an amazing game for us, and we all felt we had to do the same for him. Sometimes in special circumstances, you make special plays. I think it's fair to say we were inspired by Irv."

Brett told a reporter, "I knew that my dad would have wanted me to play. I love him so much and I love this game. . . . I know he was watching tonight."

The win over Oakland, and a week 17 thrashing of the Denver Broncos, propelled the Packers into the playoffs. On January 4, 2004, Green Bay hosted the Seattle Seahawks in a wild card game. Brett completed 26 of 38 passes for 319 yards, with a touchdown and no interceptions. But it was a defensive play that proved to be the difference in the game. In overtime, Packers cornerback Al Harris intercepted a pass by Seattle QB Matt Hasselback and took the ball 52 yards for a touchdown, giving Green Bay a 33–27 win.

In the divisional playoffs the following week, however, it was Brett Favre who threw a costly interception in overtime. The pick, by Philadelphia Eagles safety Brian Dawkins, set up a field goal that gave the Birds a 20–17 victory and ended the Packers' season.

Deanna Favre Hope Foundation > Home

http://www.deannafavre4hope.com/

Deanna Favre Hope Foundation

DEANNA FAVRE HOPE FOUNDATION

Home

About the Hope Foundation

Hope Foundation Shop

News & Events

Blog

Photo Gallery

Grant Information

Corporate Partner 4 Hope

About Breast Cancer

Beating Breast Cancer

Archive

Contact Deanna

Dear Friends,

Brett and I enjoyed our time with family and friends this past summer. We thought this new slower paced life would continue, but the phone rang, the Vikings called, and Brett just couldn't sit still!

During the summer, Brett and I took time to reflect on the work of our two foundations. We are both so proud that our foundations have been able to donate over $4 million dollars in grants to charities focused on improving the quality of life for disadvantaged and disabled children and to individuals undergoing breast cancer treatment in Wisconsin and Mississippi. It has been the support of fans and friends that enabled us to carry out our mission. Without hesitation, we both agree it is important for us to continue our efforts. The need continues to be great in our areas of focus.

To spend our time and efforts wisely and ensure our outreach remains focused and efficient, we have decided to combine our two charities. Currently both Foundations have discontinued accepting grants until the merger is complete. We ask that you be patient with us during this time of change and to please keep checking back on our website for updates on our progress.

It is our faith in God, the support from family and friends, and the many blessings we have enjoyed in our life that encourage us to maintain our commitment to those in need.

God Bless.

Sincerely,
Deanna Favre
CEO/PRESIDENT
DEANNA FAVRE HOPE FOUNDATION

DEANNA FAVRE
Don't bet against me!

HOW CAN I HELP?

Checkout our new store and help support the Foundation!

Go! »

SHANE STANFORD

FINDING HOPE when your CIRCUMSTANCES SEEM IMPOSSIBLE

WHEN GOD DISAPPEARS

SHANE STANFORD

Please visit my friend Shane Stanford site and check out his book.

Learn More »

NEWS & EVENTS

There are a lot of great things happening, see our past news and events and keep checking back to see what we have coming up!

Go There »

©2010 Deanna Favre Hope Foundation

created using: buildmyownsite.com

After Deanna completed her cancer treatments, she and Brett established the Deanna Favre Hope Foundation. This organization's mission is to help women who have been diagnosed with breast cancer but cannot afford treatment.

Twin Tragedies

The 2004 football season was barely a month old when the Favres were devastated by a terrible tragedy. On October 6, Casey Tynes, Deanna's 24-year-old brother, was killed in an all-terrain-vehicle accident. Like Brett, Casey had struggled with addiction. But he had recently gotten his life on track and was eagerly anticipating the birth of his first child.

Less than a week after Casey's funeral, while the Favres were still numb with grief, they received more awful news: Deanna was diagnosed with breast cancer. "The walls seemed like they were caving in," Brett would recall. His first thought, he admitted, was to quit football immediately. Ultimately the Favres decided that Brett should complete the season.

Deanna had surgery and began **chemotherapy** treatments, and Brett did his best to keep her spirits up. "He was so supportive," Deanna would recall.

> **"He was a big shoulder for me to cry on. I'm not a crier, I never do that. And he would come in in the evening and I would be bawling and he didn't quite know what to do. But he was very sensitive and he listened and he just talked me through it."**

At home, Brett tried to sound optimistic—just as he continued trying to fulfill his role as the Packers' team leader. But in both cases, he would confess, it was mostly just acting. He was filled with fear about what would happen to Deanna, and, he later said, "the last thing I wanted to do was come to the stadium and study for the opposing team."

Somehow, though, Brett put together a good season, throwing 30 touchdown passes and leading the Packers to a first-place finish in the NFC North Division. But in the wild card round of the playoffs, against Minnesota, Brett came up short. He threw four interceptions, and the Vikings won, 31–17.

As far as Brett was concerned, his football career was now over. "For three months I was 100% sure I was not coming back," he recalled.

"My wife was still going through her [chemo-therapy] treatments, and I was more concerned about that than she was. It was making her sick, but she was saying, 'You need to go back. You don't want to finish on a note like that.'"

Brett said the Minnesota game wouldn't define his career. But Deanna pressed. "I told him," she later revealed, "it was his decision . . . but selfishly I would like you to go back. After losing his dad and losing my brother, it just seemed we hadn't enjoyed those two seasons, and I would like to enjoy at least one more year."

And so Brett Favre, age 35, decided to return for one more season.

RECORD BREAKER

B y the summer of 2005, as Brett prepared for his 15th season in the NFL, a semblance of normalcy was returning to the Favre household. Deanna had completed her chemotherapy treatments, and in June her doctors pronounced her cancer free. Deanna's experience prompted her to try to help other women facing the disease.

Football Frustrations

Brett had returned to the Packers so that Deanna could enjoy one last football season. But in 2005, there wasn't a whole lot to enjoy. The Packers staggered to a 4–12 record, the team's worst mark since 1991. And Brett suffered his worst season. He threw a career-high 29 interceptions (with only 20 touchdown passes). He also recorded a

passer rating of 70.9—the lowest of his career, outside of his blink-of-an-eye rookie action with the Atlanta Falcons.

If the playoff loss to Minnesota would have been an unfortunate way to end a glorious career, the 2005 season would have made an even uglier swan song. Brett decided to come back for another year.

The Packers' 2006 campaign picked up where their dreary 2005 season had ended. In the season opener, a home game against the Chicago Bears, Brett connected on just 15 of 29 pass attempts for a paltry 170 yards, with no touchdowns and two interceptions. And to the dismay of the Cheeseheads at Lambeau, the Packers suffered a 26–0 whitewashing at the hands of their NFC North rivals.

Green Bay proceeded to lose 8 of its first 12 games before putting together a 4-game winning streak to finish the season at 8–8. For the second straight year, however, the Packers missed the playoffs.

Brett's individual stats were better than they had been in 2005, though by any measure it was a subpar year for him. He threw an equal number of touchdowns and interceptions (18), and at 72.7 his 2006 passer rating was among the lowest in his career.

Week 15 of the 2006 season did bring one career highlight, however. Right before halftime in the game against the Detroit Lions, Brett fired a 21-yard pass to wide receiver Carlyle Holiday. It was Brett's 4,968th pass completion, breaking the NFL career record previously held by Dan Marino of the Miami Dolphins. When asked after the game about the milestone, Brett wasn't in a self-congratulatory mood. "I'm more

Brett reacts after throwing an interception during a 2006 game against the Chicago Bears. The quarterback's troubles, and the Packers' losses, during 2005 and 2006 made some people think it was time for Brett to retire.

concerned about the three I completed to their team," he said, referring to the three interceptions he had thrown.

The Packers' final game of 2006 was a 26–7 thrashing of the NFC's first-place team, the Chicago Bears. Interviewed as he walked off the field, Brett seemed to signal that he was ready to hang up his cleats. With tears streaming down his cheeks, he said:

CROSS-CURRENTS

Brett and Deanna Favre have given a lot back to the community. For information about the Favres' charitable work, turn to page 54.

❝If this is my last game, I want to remember it. It's tough. I love these guys. I love this game. What a great way to go out against a great football team. I couldn't ask for a better way to get out.❞

During the early weeks of the new year, however, Brett began to waver. Eventually, with his 38th birthday looming, he decided to return to Green Bay for his 17th NFL season. Many sportswriters and football commentators—and even some Cheeseheads—thought this would prove to be an unfortunate decision.

Revival

Good times returned to Green Bay in 2007, as the Packers won nine more games than they had in 2006. Perhaps the biggest reason for the turnaround was a rejuvenated Brett Favre. In 2007, Brett—who would be voted to his ninth Pro Bowl—notched 28 touchdowns while getting picked only 15 times. He completed 66.5 percent of his pass attempts, a career best to that point. He threw for 4,155 total yards and averaged nearly 260 passing yards per game—his highest numbers in both of those categories since 1998.

In the 2007 season opener, the Packers slipped by the Philadelphia Eagles, 16–13. Then, paced by Brett's three touchdown passes, Green Bay spanked the New York Giants, 35–13, in week 2. The victory was the 149th of Brett's career, moving him past John Elway as the winningest quarterback in NFL history. In a postgame interview, Brett downplayed the record's significance. He said:

❝I've always been about the team. That hasn't changed. I think it's unfair that the quarterback gets labeled with wins and losses. I think it's a team effort.❞

Green Bay fans celebrate Brett's record-breaking 422nd career NFL touchdown pass, September 30, 2007. That day Brett completed 32 of 45 passes (71 percent) for 344 yards and two scores, leading Green Bay to a 23–16 win over the Vikings.

The team continued to win, beating the San Diego Chargers in week 3 and the Minnesota Vikings in week 4. In the first quarter of the game against Minnesota, Brett found wide receiver Greg Jennings for a 16-yard score. It was Brett's 421st career touchdown pass, tying him with Dan Marino for the NFL record. In the fourth quarter, Brett claimed sole possession of the record with a 33-yard rocket to rookie wideout James Jones.

In week 5, Brett and his teammates stumbled, dropping a 27–20 decision to the Chicago Bears. But then the Packers reeled off six straight wins. They finished atop the NFC North Division with a record of 13–3. Along the way, Brett added another individual record to his résumé. On December 16, in the fourth quarter of Green Bay's week 15 matchup with the St. Louis Rams, Brett found veteran wide receiver Donald Driver over the middle for a seven-yard gain. The play broke Dan Marino's record for most career passing yards.

Brett was humble about his achievement. After the game, he told reporters:

Brett announces his retirement at a press conference on March 6, 2008, at Lambeau Field.

❝I've said this all along and will continue to say it, I've never considered myself in the same league as Dan Marino. What a great passer, maybe the greatest passer ever. . . . [T]o be mentioned in the same breath with him is quite an honor.❞

Of all his individual records, Brett noted, "I would much rather win."

Brett got his wish in the divisional playoffs. On January 12, 2008, the Packers manhandled the Seattle Seahawks, 42–20, at Lambeau Field. With the victory, Green Bay advanced to the NFC championship game.

On January 20, Green Bay hosted the New York Giants, a team the Packers had demolished in week 2. From early on, however, it was clear that the conference championship game would be no cakewalk. When the game clock wound down to 0:00 in the fourth quarter, the score was knotted at 20.

The Packers won the coin flip and received the ball to start the overtime. But on the second play from scrimmage, Brett tried to force a pass to Donald Driver. It was picked off by New York cornerback

Corey Webster, setting up a field goal that ended Green Bay's season and propelled the Giants into the Super Bowl.

Decisions . . . and Revisions

In early March 2008, Brett Favre informed Packers team management that he had decided to retire from football. Team officials lavished praise on the only starting quarterback Green Bay had known for the previous 16 years, and the tributes echoed from every corner of the NFL. Players, coaches, general managers, and announcers lauded Brett's skill, toughness, competitiveness, and enthusiasm.

At a March 6 press conference at Lambeau Field—as he thanked coaches, teammates, and the people of Green Bay—Brett at times could not fight back the tears. But, he said, "As I look back on my career, no regrets. No regrets whatsoever."

Soon, however, Brett began to feel the urge to play football again. In June, he contacted the Packers about attending training camp. But head coach Mike McCarthy and other team officials weren't interested in having Brett back. The Packers had committed to 24-year-old Aaron Rodgers as their quarterback of the future.

What followed was a swirl of controversy. Brett asked Green Bay to release him from his contract. The team refused. The Packers offered to pay Brett—reportedly $2 million per year for 10 years—to work with the organization's marketing department. He wasn't interested. In late July, Brett filed a formal request with NFL commissioner Roger Goodell to be reinstated to the league. This left the Packers with only three choices: accept Brett back on the team, release him, or

Jets fans were excited when Brett was traded to New York before the start of the 2008 season. By late November, Brett had led the Jets to an 8–3 record, and the team was on track to earn an AFC playoff spot. However, the Jets lost four of their last five games and missed the postseason.

trade him. The team chose the last option. On August 6, Brett was sent to the AFC's New York Jets for a future draft pick.

When he arrived in New York, Brett made it clear that he had one goal: to help the Jets—who had suffered through a 4–12 season in 2007—win. While the team did collect five more victories with Brett taking the snaps, the 2008 season wasn't exactly a storybook affair. With a 9–7 record, the Jets missed the playoffs.

Brett had played inconsistently. His league-high 22 interceptions matched the number of touchdown passes he threw. Down the stretch especially, Brett was unable to summon any of the magic his fans had been accustomed to seeing. Much of that may have had to do with a torn biceps muscle Brett had suffered. But in any event, he threw nine interceptions in the last five games of the season, and New York lost four of those games.

In February 2009, Brett informed Jets management on a conference call that he had decided to retire—for real. "It's time to leave," he said.

Turning Back the Clock

Brett's second retirement lasted about as long as his first. In August 2009, he signed a two-year contract with the Minnesota Vikings.

For Cheeseheads, this turn of events was almost unthinkable. It had been bad enough to see Brett in a Jets uniform, but at least he had been in the AFC. Now he would be playing in the same conference and division as the Packers, the NFC North. Brett would face his former team twice during the regular season. The first meeting came in week 4, when the 2–1 Packers traveled to the Metrodome in Minneapolis to face the undefeated Vikings. A *Monday Night Football* audience saw Brett scorch Green Bay's defense with three touchdown passes and lead Minnesota to a 30–23 victory.

By the time Green Bay and Minnesota faced off for the second time, in week 8, Brett was in the midst of a truly amazing season, and the Vikings sported a 6–1 record. The Cheeseheads weren't feeling much love for Brett at his Lambeau Field homecoming. He was booed loudly and repeatedly. Brett claimed he understood—"Packer fans cheer for the Packers first," he said—and he didn't let the unfriendly welcome affect his performance. Brett completed 17 of 28 passes for 244 yards, with

CROSS-CURRENTS

On September 20, 2009, Brett Favre set a new NFL record for most consecutive starts by a player at any position. To find out whose record Brett broke, see page 55.

four touchdowns and no interceptions. The Vikings left Lambeau with a 38–26 win.

Throughout 2009, the 40-year-old quarterback played as if he'd found the fountain of youth. He finished the regular season with 33 touchdown passes and only 7 picks, the lowest interception total of his career. His 68.4 completion percentage was a career best, as was his passer rating of 107.2. Minnesota, meanwhile, compiled a record of 12–4, finished atop the NFC North Division, and smoked the Dallas Cowboys, 34–3, in the divisional playoffs.

The NFC championship game pitted the Vikings against the New Orleans Saints. Played at the Louisiana Superdome on January 24, 2010, the game was a seesaw struggle. With 2:37 left in the fourth quarter and the score deadlocked at 28, Minnesota got the ball at its own 21-yard line after a Saints punt. Brett drove his team downfield. With 19 seconds left, the ball sat at the Saints' 38-yard line. Facing third-and-15, Brett took the snap and rolled to his right. It appeared he had room to run for six or seven yards—enough to get the Vikings within field goal range. But Brett elected to throw a difficult pass, across his body and to the middle of the field. He was looking for Sidney Rice, but the pass was intercepted by Saints cornerback Tracy Porter. The quarter expired with the game still tied, and New Orleans won the game in overtime with a field goal.

It was a heartbreaking end to an amazing season. But would it be Brett Favre's last hurrah on the gridiron? As winter gave way to spring in 2010, Brett wasn't saying—and no one seemed ready to count him out. After all, every time he has been knocked down—on or off the football field—Brett has gotten back up. And even after 19 years in the NFL, he continues to display a kid's joy in playing the game.

Conferences and Divisions

The 32 teams in the National Football League (NFL) are divided into two conferences: the National Football Conference (NFC) and the American Football Conference (AFC). Each conference has 16 teams. The conferences are also split into four divisions of four teams each. The NFC includes the NFC North, the NFC East, the NFC West, and the NFC South, and the AFC's four divisions are also called North, East, West, and South.

Playoffs

The divisions and conferences have two main purposes. One is to help determine which teams make the playoffs, sometimes called the postseason. Playoff games are held after the regular season ends. They match the best teams in each conference. Teams that lose are out of the competition. The playoffs end with the Super Bowl, which determines the league champion.

The four division winners in each conference automatically make the playoffs. In 2009, for instance, Brett and the Minnesota Vikings won the NFC North, so they moved on to the postseason. Each conference also sends two other teams to the playoffs. These teams are known as wild cards. They are the teams that had the best records without winning their divisions. The NFC wild card teams in 2009 were the Green Bay Packers and Philadelphia Eagles.

In the first few games of the postseason, teams play other teams in their own conference. This system produces a champion for each conference. These two teams then meet in the Super Bowl. As a result, the Super Bowl is always between the AFC champion and the NFC champion. The 2009 season ended with the NFC champion New Orleans Saints beating the Indianapolis Colts, who won the AFC.

Schedule

The conferences and divisions are also used to plan schedules. Each year teams play two games against other teams in their own division. In the NFC North, for example, the Vikings play two games each against Detroit, Chicago, and Green Bay. Teams also play six games against teams that are in their conference, but not in their division. In 2009 the Vikings played the NFC West teams Arizona, St. Louis, San Francisco, and Seattle, along with Carolina (NFC South) and the New York Giants (NFC East).

Finally, teams play four games against teams in the other conference. The 2009 Vikings took on the teams of the AFC North—Baltimore, Cincinnati, Cleveland, and Pittsburgh. In this way teams play most of their games against division rivals and other teams in their own conference. But they also get a chance to compare themselves to the clubs in the other conference. (Go back to page 5.) ◂◂

Bear Bryant

In the history of college football, only a handful of people have come close to making as great an impact as Paul Bryant, longtime coach of the University of Alabama. "His nickname," remarked Hall of Fame quarterback Joe Namath, who played for Bryant at Alabama, "was Bear. Now imagine a guy that can carry the nickname Bear." Bryant certainly lived up to the nickname. As a college lineman at Alabama, he once played a game with a broken leg.

Paul "Bear" Bryant was born in Moro Bottom, Arkansas, on September 11, 1913. He acquired his nickname as a 13-year-old, when he was bitten on the ear while wrestling a carnival bear for one dollar.

After playing football at Alabama, Bryant was an assistant coach there and at Vanderbilt University before landing his first head-coaching job, at the University of Kentucky, in 1946. He remained at Kentucky until 1954, when he became the head coach at Texas A&M.

The Bear returned to Alabama as head coach in 1958. He soon transformed the Crimson Tide into college football's most dominant team. Beginning in 1959, Alabama appeared in postseason bowl games 24 years in a row. The Crimson Tide won national titles in 1961, 1964, 1965, 1978, and 1979. Bryant retired after the 1982 season as the winningest head coach in college football history, with an amazing 323 victories against just 85 losses and 17 ties. Sadly, he didn't get to enjoy his retirement. On January 26, 1983, just 28 days after coaching his final game, Bear Bryant died of heart failure at the age of 69.

"Even his peers in the coaching business felt in awe of him," noted Penn State's Joe Paterno, who, along with Florida State's Bobby Bowden, would eventually amass more lifetime coaching victories than Bear Bryant. "He had such charisma. He was just a giant figure." (Go back to page 14.)◀◀

QB Miscalculations: The 1991 Draft

Each year the NFL conducts what is officially termed a *player selection meeting,* commonly called the draft. This is the process by which the NFL brings into the league new players from the ranks of college football.

The draft, which takes place near the end of April, is organized into a series of seven rounds. In every round, each of the NFL's 32 teams gets to pick a player. The order in which teams pick is determined by their success the previous year. The team with the worst record gets the first choice, the team with the second-worst record gets the second choice, and so on. The Super Bowl winner gets the last pick of the round. The draft is organized this way in order to balance the talent levels among the teams. Teams can change the order of their picks, however, through trades.

Because a team's long-term success depends on continually acquiring top players, all of the NFL's franchises spend a lot of time and effort preparing for the annual draft. Each year, teams compile enormous files on college prospects. Before the draft, highly regarded college players are put through a series of physical and psychological tests.

In most cases, this homework pays off. A recent study of All-Pro players over the previous five seasons found that half were drafted in the first round.

Sometimes, however, teams overlook a college player who goes on to have a great NFL career. Such was the case in 1991. That year, the Dallas Cowboys took defensive tackle Russell Maryland with the first overall pick. In all, 32 players—including two quarterbacks—were drafted before the Atlanta Falcons chose Brett Favre in the second round.

The top quarterback in the 1991 draft was San Diego State's Dan McGwire. The Seattle Seahawks selected him in the first round, with the 16th overall pick. McGwire's NFL career consisted of four seasons with the Seahawks and one with the Miami Dolphins. During that time, he played in a total of 13 games, 5 of which he started. McGwire finished his pro career with 745 passing yards, two touchdown passes, and six interceptions.

The other quarterback chosen in the first round of the 1991 draft, Todd Marinovich, was an even bigger bust. Marinovich, who entered the draft after his sophomore season at the University of Southern California, was selected by the Oakland Raiders with the 24th overall pick. Plagued by drug problems, Marinovich was out of football by 1993. In his two seasons with the Raiders, he played in just eight games and threw for a total of 1,345 yards, with eight touchdown passes and nine interceptions.

Through the 2009 season, Brett Favre's career passing yardage exceeded that of McGwire and Marinovich combined by a mere 67,239 yards—38.2

miles. Brett had also thrown for 487 more touchdowns than the combined total of the first two quarterbacks selected in the 1991 draft. Needless to say, a host of NFL general managers and coaches rued the day they overlooked the quarterback from Southern Mississippi. (Go back to page 21.)◀◀

A Unique Franchise

Located in northeastern Wisconsin, along the shores of an inlet of Lake Michigan, Green Bay is a city of just over 100,000 residents. That might seem too small a population to provide an adequate fan base for an NFL franchise. But Packers fans are an extraordinarily devoted bunch. And the team is unlike any other franchise in football—or, for that matter, in all of American professional sports. The Packers aren't owned by an individual or by a small group of investors. Since 1923, the team has been owned by its fans, through shares of stock.

Today, there are some 112,000 shareholders in Green Bay Packers, Inc. The majority are residents of Wisconsin, but all 50 states are represented among the corporation's shareholders. Shares confer voting rights, but no dividends are ever paid, the price of the stock doesn't increase, and shares may only be resold to Green Bay Packers, Inc. In addition, no individual may own more than 200,000 of the approximately 4.75 million shares. The rules are designed to ensure that no one can take over the Packers—and that the club will always remain in Green Bay. (Go back to page 22.)◀◀

The retired numbers of great players from Packers history are posted above the north end zone at Green Bay's historic Lambeau Field.

The Pro Bowl

The NFL is the only major professional sports league that holds its annual all-star game after the regular season ends. Major League Baseball, the National Basketball Association, and the National Hockey League hold their all-star games in the middle of their seasons.

The first NFL-sponsored all-star game was played in early 1939, after the end of the 1938 season. The NFL champions, the New York Giants, beat a collection of all-stars from other NFL teams and two independent teams, 13–10. This version of the game, with the NFL champion playing a group of all-stars, continued for four years until World War II interrupted the NFL's play.

The all-star game resumed in 1950 and pitted the all-stars of the NFL's American Conference against the all-stars of the National Conference. After the NFL was realigned into East and West divisions in 1953, the game matched up the best players in the East with the best in the West. That arrangement continued until the NFL formally merged with the American Football League (AFL) in 1970. The game, now called the Pro Bowl, became a matchup between the best players in the NFL's two divisions, the American Football Conference (AFC) and National Football Conference (NFC).

Three groups—the fans, players, and coaches—vote on who will play for the NFC and AFC in the Pro Bowl. Each group has one-third of the voting power, to prevent fans of one team or one particular player from dominating the vote. Before 1995, only coaches and players were allowed to vote.

Between 1980 and 2009, the Pro Bowl was always played at Aloha Stadium in Honolulu, Hawaii, on the Sunday after the Super Bowl. However, several changes were made before the 2010 Pro Bowl. The game was moved to Dolphin Stadium in South Florida. Also, it was moved to the Sunday before Super Bowl XLIV. NFL officials said that these changes would increase fan interest in the all-star exhibition. However, the changes meant that Pro Bowl players on the two Super Bowl teams could not participate in the game for fear of injury.

The game has grown into a weeklong celebration. The week before the game, there are numerous parties, an NFL alumni touch football game, a celebrity golf tournament, and a football skills contest. Some players look forward to the Pro Bowl as a postseason vacation. Others feel honored to be selected but choose not to play, so they can rest and recover from the long NFL season. (Go back to page 23.)◀◀

The Super Bowl

Although the first Super Bowl was played in 1967, its roots go back to 1960, when the American Football League (AFL) was formed to compete with the long-established National Football League (NFL). The AFL quickly became a strong rival to the older league.

By the mid-1960s, owners in both leagues were concerned that the competition between them was driving the players' salaries too high. The owners decided to merge the two leagues and form a single league. It would take several years to work out the details of the merger. One of the conditions, however, was that the winner of one league would play the winner of the other in a championship game.

The NFL's Most Famous Ball

At first, Pete Rozelle, the head of the NFL, wanted to call this game "The Big One." Then one day, Kansas City Chiefs owner Lamar Hunt came up with a different name. He was watching his children play with a Super Ball, and that toy gave him the idea of calling the game the "Super Bowl." He doubted this nickname would last very long, but he was wrong. Today, the Super Ball that the Hunt children played with is in the Professional Football Hall of Fame.

In the first Super Bowl in 1967, the Green Bay Packers easily defeated Lamar Hunt's Kansas City Chiefs, 35–10. The game's result was nearly the same the following year, with a 33–14 Packer win over the Oakland Raiders. These two wins seemed to confirm many fans' beliefs that the NFL had a higher quality of play.

The Namath Guarantee

In 1969, nearly everyone expected the third game to follow the same pattern. The NFL's Baltimore Colts were 18-point favorites over the AFL's New York Jets. Jets quarterback Joe Namath, however, guaranteed that his team would win. He backed up his words on the field, and his team emerged with a 16–7 win, one of the greatest upsets in American sports history. When the AFL champion Chiefs defeated the NFL champion Minnesota Vikings 23–7 the following year, doubts about the competitive differences between the leagues disappeared.

By the start of the 1970 season, the merger was complete. The new league was known as the National Football League. Its then-26 teams were divided into two conferences: the American Football Conference (AFC), which consisted of 10 AFL teams plus 3 former NFL teams, and the National Football Conference (NFC), which consisted of the 13 remaining NFL teams. From then on, the Super Bowl would match the two conference winners.

Today, the Super Bowl is the single most-watched television event in the United States. Super Bowl Sunday has almost become a national holiday. (Go back to page 26.) ◀◀

Money and the NFL

In the early days of professional football, players took the field for little more than a "sawbuck" —$10—and a pat on the back. But over the last 30 years, with the arrival of players unions and televised games, salaries have skyrocketed.

In 1994, in an effort to slow the rise in player salaries and to help owners control costs, the NFL put in place a salary cap for its players. This means that no team can spend more than a specified amount of money to pay the salaries of all the players on its roster. At the outset, the cap was set at $34.6 million annually. The cap is adjusted each year based on the amount of money the NFL earns. As of 2008 it stood at $116 million.

To afford their high-performing playmakers, team presidents craft complex contracts, which typically include bonuses, options, and deferred payments that spread costs out over a number of years in order to allow the team to meet a given year's salary cap. For the 2008 season, Pittsburgh Steelers quarterback Ben Roethlisberger was the highest-paid player in the NFL, making $27.7 million in compensation that would count toward the salary cap. That worked out to about $1.45 million per game, including the postseason. The second-highest-paid player for 2008 was defensive end Jared Allen of the Minnesota Vikings, who received about $21.1 million. Wide receiver Larry Fitzgerald of the Arizona Cardinals was third on the 2008 money list, taking in $17.1 million. Rounding out the top five were second-year Oakland Raiders quarterback JaMarcus Russell, whose $16.8 million in compensation seemed way out of balance with his mediocre performance; and running back Michael Turner, whom the Atlanta Falcons signed as a free agent for $16 million.

Of course, the average NFL salary is considerably lower. The minimum salary for an NFL rookie in 2008 was $295,000. Each year of experience in the league guarantees a larger minimum salary.

Still, payroll costs for NFL teams are enormous. About two-thirds of all revenue generated by NFL teams each year goes to the players. In May 2008, NFL commissioner Roger Goodell announced that the league might extend the 16-game season by one game to increase team owners' profits. (Go back to page 31.) ◀◀

Giving Back

Brett and Deanna Favre have often remarked about how lucky they consider themselves. The couple has done a great deal to help those who haven't been so fortunate.

Brett has long donated his time to the Make-A-Wish Foundation, an organization that grants the wishes of children facing life-threatening medical conditions. As a Make-A-Wish volunteer, Brett has met, thrown the football around with, and escorted dozens of kids to team practices, meals, and the like. "It's an honor to be asked, but I'm not going to lie—it's hard," he says of the experience. "There are times when it takes a lot out of me. These kids are so cool, but you can't ignore what they're up against and what their families are going through."

In 1996, Brett and Deanna established the Brett Favre Fourward Foundation. Inspired by Brett's mother, who was a special-education teacher for many years, the Fourward Foundation helps disabled and disadvantaged kids in Mississippi and Wisconsin. Over the years it has donated more than $3 million to various groups in those two states. The Fourward Foundation also raised $1 million to help the victims of 2005's Hurricane Katrina, which devastated the Gulf Coast.

After her experience with breast cancer, Deanna Favre wanted to help other women facing the disease. She and Brett established a second major charitable organization, the Deanna Favre Hope Foundation. It raises money to pay for the cancer treatments of uninsured women. "I was shocked," Deanna said, "by how much it cost to have my cancer treatment. I don't like the spotlight, but I want to help people." (Go back to page 40.) ◀◀

Web site of the Brett Favre Fourward Foundation, which raises money for children's charities in Mississippi and Wisconsin.

Jim Marshall: NFL Iron Man

Football is a tough, violent game. In the NFL, injuries are a fact of life, and at some point in his career almost every player misses games because he is hurt. Jim Marshall wasn't almost every player. When he retired at the end of the 1979 season, Marshall—a 6'4", 248-pound defensive end—had started every game for the previous 19 seasons. His amazing streak of 270 consecutive starts was an NFL record that stood for almost 30 years. On September 20, 2009, Brett Favre made his 271st consecutive start, pushing Marshall to number two on the NFL's list of all-time iron men.

Born in Danville, Kentucky, in 1937, Jim Marshall played college football at Ohio State University. He left Ohio State after his junior year and was picked by the Cleveland Browns in the fourth round of the 1960 NFL draft.

In 1961, after one season with Cleveland, Marshall was sent to the Minnesota Vikings, an expansion team in its first year of operation. There he remained for the rest of his career.

Marshall was selected to the Pro Bowl in 1968 and 1969, and he helped anchor one of the most feared defensive lines ever. Nicknamed the "Purple People Eaters," that line powered the Vikings to four Super Bowl appearances between 1970 and 1977. The team never won the big game, however.

In 1979, Marshall retired not only with the career record for consecutive starts but also with the career record for fumbles recovered, 29. One of those fumble recoveries also set two NFL records, albeit ones Jim Marshall would just as soon have forgotten. On October 25, 1964, Marshall picked up a San Francisco 49ers fumble at the Vikings' 34-yard line. He rumbled 66 yards to the end zone, where he tossed the ball into the stands in celebration. Unfortunately, Marshall had run the wrong way, and the play went for −66 yards and a safety—the shortest play and the longest safety in NFL history. (Go back to page 44.) ◄◄

1969 Brett Lorenzo Favre is born in Gulfport, Mississippi, on October 10.

1983 Enters Hancock North Central High School.

1987 Enters the University of Southern Mississippi on a football scholarship. Becomes the Golden Eagles' starting quarterback in the third game of his freshman year.

1989 Brett's girlfriend, Deanna Tynes, gives birth to a daughter, Brittany. Brett leads Southern Miss to a stunning upset victory over the sixth-ranked Florida State Seminoles.

1990 Nearly dies in a July 14 car accident.

1991 Selected by the Atlanta Falcons in the second round of the NFL draft.

1992 In February, is traded by the Falcons to the Green Bay Packers. During week 3 of the 1992 season, replaces injured starter Don Majkowski.

1995 After leading league in touchdown passes (38) and passing yards (4,413), wins his first NFL MVP award.

1996 In May, announces that he is addicted to painkillers and enters a rehabilitation clinic. Marries Deanna Tynes in July. Establishes the Brett Favre Fourward Foundation, which supports charities in Mississippi and Wisconsin. Wins his second consecutive MVP award.

1997 On January 26, leads the Packers to a 35–21 victory over the New England Patriots in Super Bowl XXXI. In July, signs a seven-year contract with Green Bay worth up to $48 million. Wins third straight MVP award.

1998 Packers win NFC championship but lose to the Denver Broncos in Super Bowl XXXII. Brett has a cameo role in the motion-picture comedy *There's Something About Mary.*

1999 Brett enters rehab for alcohol dependency. Deanna gives birth to another daughter, Breleigh, in July.

2001 Signs a 10-year deal with the Packers worth $100 million.

2003 Father, Irvin, dies on December 21; Brett has a phenomenal Monday night game on December 22.

2004 In October, Deanna's brother is killed in an accident, and Deanna is diagnosed with breast cancer.

2006 Breaks Dan Marino's career record for pass completions.

2007 Breaks NFL career records for most wins by a quarterback, most touchdown passes, and most passing yards. Named Sportsman of the Year by *Sports Illustrated.*

2008 In March, announces his retirement but reconsiders that decision over the summer. Packers trade Brett to the New York Jets in August.

2009 In February, Brett again announces his retirement. In August, he again comes out of retirement, signing with the Minnesota Vikings. Has one of the best seasons of his career. Breaks NFL record for most consecutive starts by a player at any position.

2010 Becomes the first 40-year-old quarterback ever to win a postseason game when Minnesota beats Dallas on January 17 in the divisional playoffs.

Year	Team	G	GS	Comp	Att	Pct	Yds	Avg	TD	Int	Rate
1991	Atlanta Falcons	2	0	0	4	0.0	0	0.0	0	2	11
1992	Green Bay Packers	15	13	302	471	64.1	3,227	6.9	18	13	85.3
1993	Green Bay Packers	16	16	318	522	60.9	3,303	6.3	19	24	72.2
1994	Green Bay Packers	16	16	363	582	62.4	3882	6.7	33	14	90.7
1995	Green Bay Packers	16	16	359	570	63.0	4413	7.7	38	13	99.5
1996	Green Bay Packers	16	16	325	543	59.9	3899	7.2	39	13	95.8
1997	Green Bay Packers	16	16	304	513	59.3	3867	7.5	35	16	92.6
1998	Green Bay Packers	16	16	347	551	63.0	4212	7.6	31	23	87.8
1999	Green Bay Packers	16	16	341	595	57.3	4091	6.9	22	23	74.7
2000	Green Bay Packers	16	16	338	580	58.3	3812	6.6	20	16	78.0
2001	Green Bay Packers	16	16	314	510	61.6	3921	7.7	32	15	94.1
2002	Green Bay Packers	16	16	341	551	61.9	3,658	6.6	27	16	85.6
2003	Green Bay Packers	16	16	308	471	65.4	3,361	7.1	32	21	90.4
2004	Green Bay Packers	16	16	346	540	64.1	4,088	7.6	30	17	92.4
2005	Green Bay Packers	16	16	372	607	61.3	3,881	6.4	20	29	70.9
2006	Green Bay Packers	16	16	343	613	56.0	3,885	6.3	18	18	72.7
2007	Green Bay Packers	16	16	356	535	66.5	4,155	7.8	28	15	95.7
2008	New York Jets	16	16	343	522	65.7	3,472	6.7	22	22	81.0
2009	Minnesota Vikings	16	16	363	531	68.4	4,202	7.9	33	7	107.2
Total		128	128	2,772	4,370	509.3	30,702	56.4	185.7	145	695.9

Awards and Accomplishments

Pro Bowl (1992, 1993, 1995, 1996, 1997, 2001, 2002, 2003, 2007, 2008, 2009)
First-team All-Pro (1995, 1996, 1997)
NFL MVP (1995, 1996, 1997)
Named to NFL's All-Decade Team (1990s)
Sports Illustrated Sportsman of the Year (2007)

NFL career records*

Most consecutive starts: **285** (including playoffs, 309)

Most regular-season wins by a starting quarterback: **169**

Most passing touchdowns: **497**

Most passing yards: **69,329**

Most completions: **6,083**

Most pass attempts: **9,811**

* **Records are through the 2009 season.**

Books

Carlson, Chuck, and Vernon Biever. *Brett Favre: America's Quarterback*. Chicago: Triumph Books, 2007.

Favre, Brett, with Chris Havel. *Favre: For the Record*. New York: Doubleday, 1997.

Favre, Deanna, with Angela Elwell Hunt. *Don't Bet Against Me!: Beating the Odds Against Breast Cancer and in Life*. Carol Stream, IL: Tyndale House Publishers, 2007.

Koestler-Grack, Rachel A. *Brett Favre*. New York: Facts On File, 2008.

Web Sites

http://www.officialbrettfavre.com/
"For the Love of the Game," Brett Favre's official Web site, features news, photos, links to the Favres' charitable foundations, and more.

http://www.nfl.com/players/brettfavre/profile?id=FAV540222
Brett Favre's stats, from the NFL's official Web site.

http://www.packers.com/
Everything a Cheesehead needs to know, from the Packers' team Web site.

http://www.brettfavre.com/main.php
This fan site, focused on Brett Favre's career with the Green Bay Packers, features a short bio, news items, a photo gallery, and more.

All-Pro—a football player voted best at his position in the entire NFL for a given season; ballots are cast by a panel of national sports-media members.

bayou—a body of water, such as a marsh, swamp, or very slow moving river, that is found especially in America's Gulf Coast region.

bomb—in football, a long pass.

chemotherapy—the use of chemicals to treat disease, especially cancer.

franchise—a professional sports team.

gridiron—a nickname for the football field.

mononucleosis—an infectious disease, caused by a virus, whose symptoms include fever, sore throat, and persistent fatigue.

passer rating—a statistic designed to measure a quarterback's passing efficiency.

pigskin—an informal name for a football.

Pro Bowl—the NFL's annual all-star game.

rehab—a program for rehabilitating people addicted to drugs or alcohol.

rookie—a player in his first year.

salary cap—a league-imposed limit on the amount of money a professional sports team may spend on player salaries each year.

veteran—a player with many years of experience.

wild card—one of two teams in each of the NFL's conferences that makes the playoffs without winning its division; the first round of the NFL playoffs.

page 5 "Yes. I love . . ." Brigid Mullen, "Q&A: Brett Favre," *SI On Campus. com*, October 19, 2007. http://sportsillustrated.cnn.com/2007/sioncampus/10/19/brigid.qa.favre/index.html

page 9 "As long as I'm out . . ." ESPN.com News Services, "Vikings Sack Romo Six Times to Advance to NFC Title Game vs. Saints," *ESPN.com*, January 17, 2010. http://sports.espn.go.com/nfl/recap?gameId=300117016

page 11 "We was wild . . ." Gary D'Amato, "Favre Was Toughened by Brothers, Dad," *Milwaukee Journal Sentinel*, September 10, 2005. http://www.jsonline.com/sports/packers/44678527.html

page 12 "He didn't even cry . . ." Tim Evans, "Brett Favre—The Person," *Brett Favre. com*. http://www.brettfavre.com/person.php

page 14 "The thing we had in common . . ." Andy Martino, "Through Triumph & Tragedy, Deanna and Brett Favre Remain a Constant," *New York Daily News*, September 20, 2008. http://www.nydailynews.com/sports/football/jets/2008/09/20/2008-09-20_through_triumph__tragedy_deanna_and_bret.html

page 16 "The first morning . . ." Gary D'Amato, "Life of the Party: Favre Caught on Quickly in College," *Milwaukee Journal Sentinel*, September 17, 2005. http://www3.jsonline.com/story/index.aspx?id=356600

page 18 "We had no idea . . ." Martino, "Through Triumph & Tragedy."

page 18 "You can call it a miracle . . ." Jimmy Traina, "Sports Illustrated Scrapbook: Brett Favre," *SI.com*. http://sportsillustrated.cnn.com/football/nfl/features/favre/timeline/

page 23 "All of a sudden . . ." Martino, "Through Triumph & Tragedy."

page 26 "We're champions today . . ." John McClain, "Packers Pelt Patriots with Big Plays, Give Titletown Another Championship," *Houston Chronicle*, January 27, 1997. http://www.chron.com/CDA/archives/archive.mpl/1997_1391858/packers-35-patriots-21-return-to-glory-packers-pel.html

page 27 "Thank God . . ." Deanna Favre with Angela Elwell Hunt, *Don't Bet Against Me!: Beating the Odds Against Breast Cancer and in Life* (Carol Stream, IL: Tyndale House Publishers, 2007), 9.

page 30 "Brett realized that if he . . ." Favre, *Don't Bet Against Me!*, 75.

page 32 "No player in the NFL . . ." Traina, "Sports Illustrated Scrapbook."

page 32 "It's not the end . . ." Arnie Stapleton, "Favre: 'I'll Be Back'," *Lundington* (MI) *Daily News*, January 22, 2003, page B3.

page 34 "I just said . . ." ESPN.com News Services, "Favre's First Half: 4 TDs, 311 Yards," *ESPN.com*, December 22, 2003. http://sports.espn.go.com/nfl/recap?gameId=231222013

page 34 "I knew that my dad . . ." "Favre's First Half."

page 36 "The walls seemed like . . ." Larry Weisman, "Deanna Favre Gives Green Bay Another Reason to Cheer," *USA Today*, October 19, 2005. http://www.usatoday.com/sports/football/nfl/packers/2005-10-19-deanna-favre-cover_x.htm

page 36 "He was so supportive . . ." Weisman, "Another Reason to Cheer."

page 36 "the last thing I wanted . . ." Weisman, "Another Reason to Cheer."

page 36 "For three months . . ." Larry Weisman, As Crowds Adore Him, Favre Yearns for Quiet," *USA Today*, August 11, 2005. http://www. usatoday.com/sports/football/nfl/ packers/2005-08-11-favre-cover-story_x.htm

page 37 "I told him it was his . . ." Weisman, "Favre Yearns for Quiet."

page 39 "I'm more concerned . . ." Associated Press, "Favre Sets Completions Record in Victory over Lions," *ESPN.com*, December 17, 2006. http://espn.go.com/nfl/ recap?gameId=261217009

page 40 "If this is my last . . ." Associated Press, "Favre's Last Stand? QB Fuels Pack Rout of No. 1 Bears," *ESPN.com*, December 31, 2006.

page 40 "I've always been about . . ." ESPN. com News Services, "Favre Now Winningest QB in NFL History After Packers' Win," *ESPN.com*, September 16, 2007. http://espn.go.com/nfl/ recap?gameId=270916019

page 42 "I've said this all along . . ." Mike Spofford, "Driver Snags Record-Breaker from Favre," *Packers. com*, December 16, 2007. http://www.packers.com/news/ stories/2007/12/16/4/

page 42 "I would much rather win," Spofford, "Driver Snags Record-Breaker from Favre," December 16, 2007.

page 43 "As I look back . . ." Drew Olson, editor, "Transcript of Brett Favre's Press Conference," *OnMilwaukee. com*, March 6, 2008. http://www. onmilwaukee.com/sports/articles/ favretranscript.html?page=1

page 44 "It's time . . ." ESPN.com News Services, "Favre: 'It's Been a Wonderful Career'," *ESPN. com*, February 13, 2009. http:// sports.espn.go.com/nfl/news/ story?id=3900850

page 44 "Packer fans cheer . . ." Associated Press, "Favre Beats Packers with 4 TDs in Return to Lambeau, *ESPN.com*, November 1, 2009. http://sports.espn.go.com/nfl/ recap?gameId=291101009

page 47 "His nickname was Bear . . ." Mike Puma, "Bear Bryant 'Simply the Best There Ever Was.' " *ESPN Classic*, 2007. http://espn.go.com/classic/ biography/s/Bryant_Bear.html

page 47 "Even his peers . . ." Puma, "Bear Bryant."

page 57 "It's an honor to be asked . . ." Alan Shipnuck, "Brett Favre: Sportsman of the Year," *Sports Illustrated*, December 10, 2007.

page 54 "I was shocked . . ." Martino, "Through Triumph & Tragedy."

Writer **H. H. Lourdes-Pitt** was born in Buenos Aires, Argentina, but spent most of her childhood in New Orleans. She closely followed Brett Favre's career, from his college days at Southern Miss through his time in Green Bay. She remains a fan, though she finds it much harder to catch Brett's games since moving back to South America. She currently lives in Montevideo, Uruguay, with her husband, Nigel.

PICTURE CREDITS